Little

Huge

Tiny

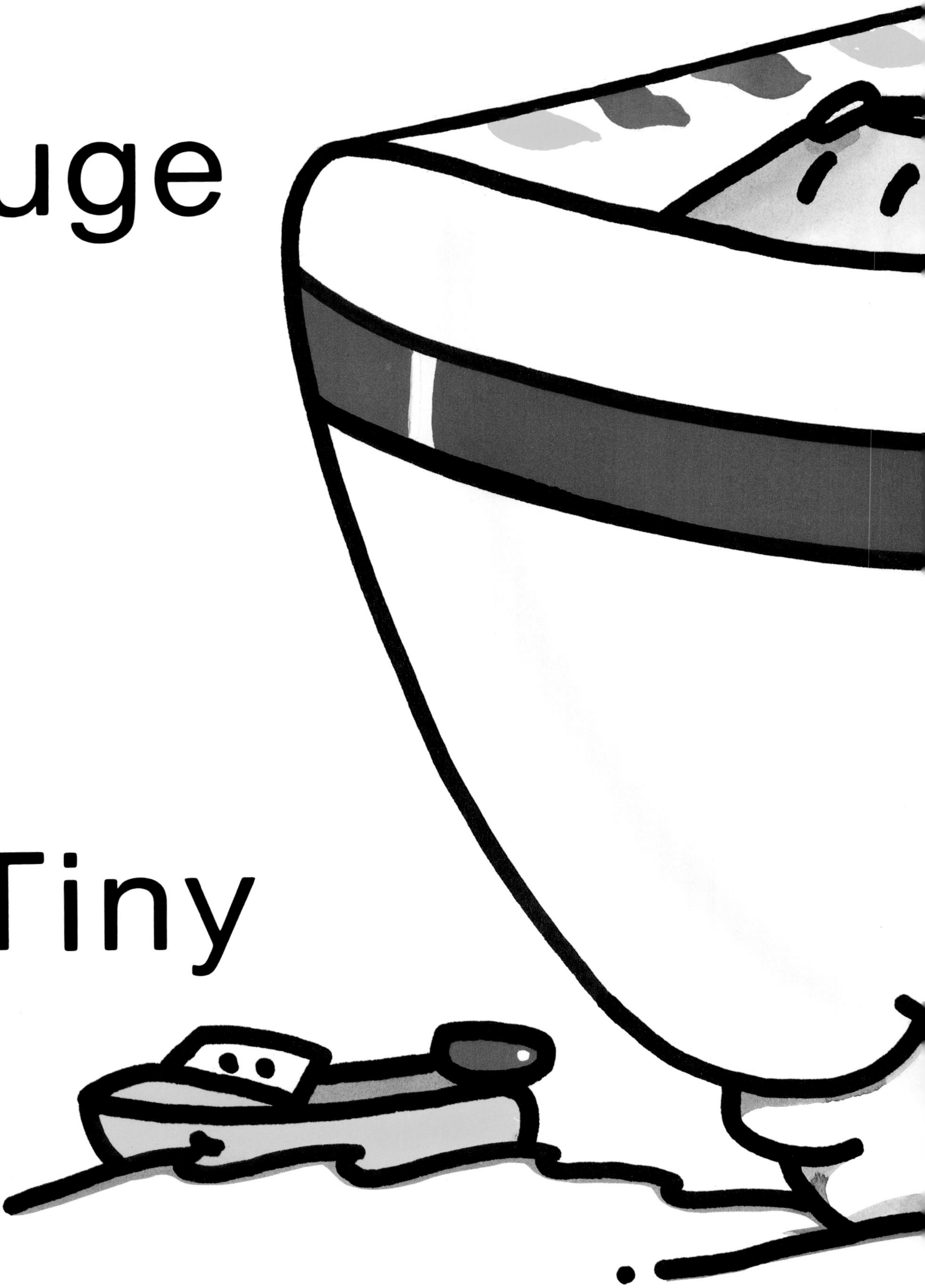

Short

Long

Big

Little

Huge

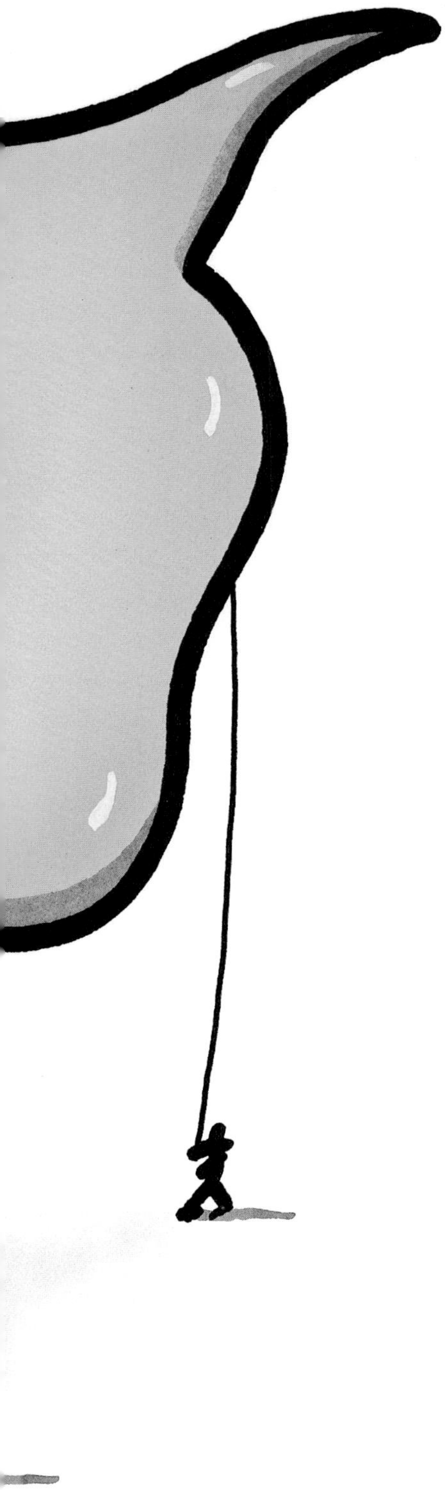

Tiny

Large

Small

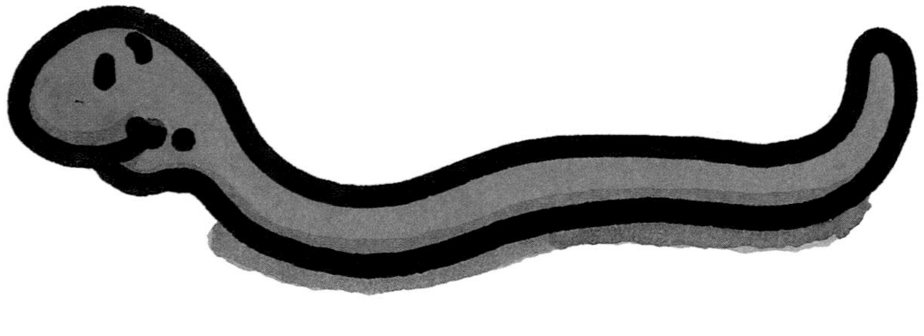

Short

Long

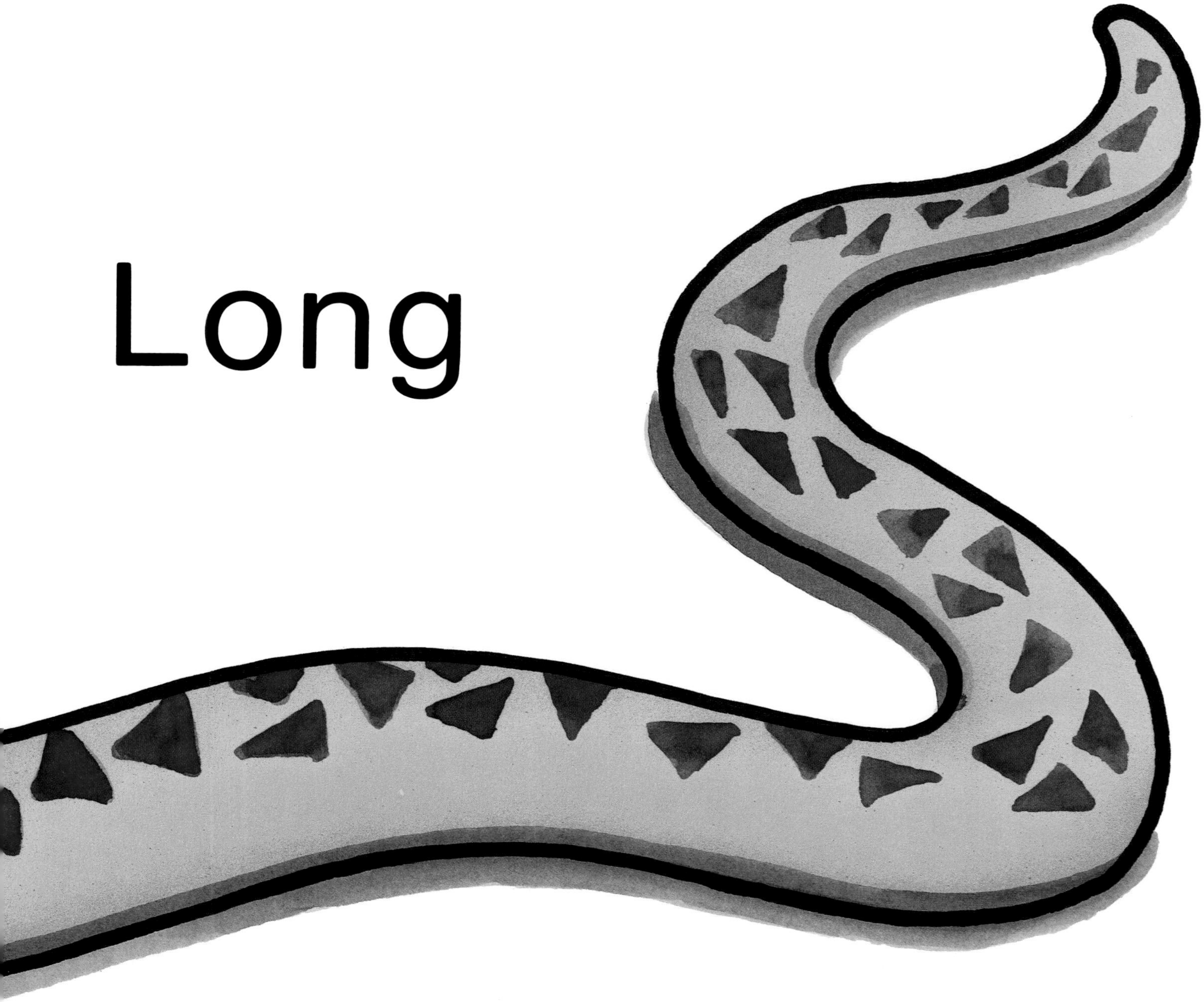

Long

Short

Tall

Short

Large

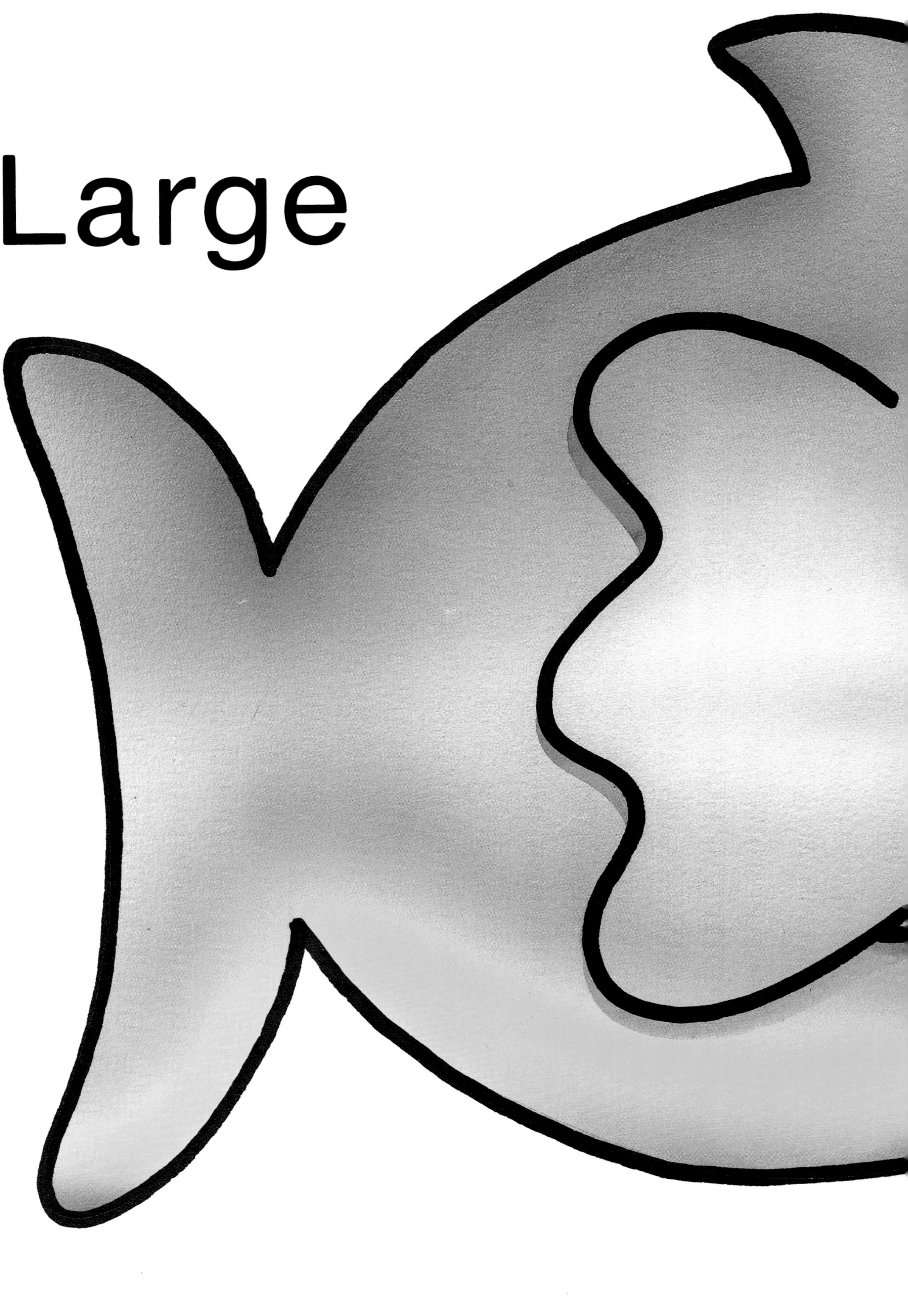

Small

Little